The

(Booklet)

Best Loved Classical Themes

Updated 2016-0901

By:

Teo (Barry) Vincent IV

To music educators and music students of the world

Teo (Barry) Vincent IV
Theme Player, Best Loved Classical Themes
p. cm.
Most loved classical favorite songs' sheet music expertly scored for piano and small ensembles, reviewed by expert professionals.
ISBN 978-1537339672 (pbk.)
1. Classical piano scores. 2. Scores for piano and voice. 3. Scores for piano with chords and guitar fretboards for the option of a wide variety of accompanists and / or soloists. 4. Scores for 2 pianists, one on piano and one on keyboard. 5. Trio Scores for small orchestra like a Chamber Orchestra for 1, 2 or 3 players.
 I. Title.
2016

Music / Genres & Styles / Classical

Teo (Barry) Vincent IV is a technical writer and composer from California. He studies at the Royal Conservatory of Music in Toronto, Canada, and piano privately with Oszkar Morzsa of the Franz Liszt Academy in Budapest, Hungary. He continues writing, composing researching, performing, recording, creating education & wellness new-media.

Teo (Barry) Vincent IV is diversity embodied. Musically there is the wild, creative and adventurous side, as in his many compositions and improvisations / impromptus. He loves to rework songs in new ways and "break the rules" of music whenever possible. On the other hand he was a top technical writer, quality control specialist stress-testing security in large accounting firms. You see this in music with an almost mechanical accuracy in rhythm. While Vincent was a technical trainer and writer in California's Silicon Valley, he also composed hundreds of his own songs, plus recorded and performed in diverse music groups including Salsa, High-Life, African, Funk, Jazz Fusion Jazz, Blues, Soul, Calypso, Zouk, Soca & more. High-Tech-Accounting-Nerd by day & Wildly-Visionary-Music-Artist by night!

Vincent's scores demonstrate his technical writing, great composition & arranging skills and love of the master composers works. When possible he includes guitar chords and guitar fretboards to allow the option of collaboration with many types of accompanists. Soloists can also use the chords to aid their improvisations, and the chords give musicians of all levels better understanding of the compositions' structures and forms.

All Vincent wishes is that more people can enjoy beautiful music with creative ways to interpret it and have fun with it!

A really big special thanks to George *"Thurgopedia"* Thurgood at the Royal Conservatory of Music for his academic excellence, expert teaching skills, piano & creative collaboration.

Thanks to Oszkar Morzsa for sharing his virtuosic finesse, piano teaching & great knowledge of music of the world.

Our Charmony Series:

1) Honoring Those That Went Before, Classical and World Music Piano Scores. 2) World Music Class, The Aspire Higher Project. 3) Vincent Trio Scores. 4) Soul + Salsa = Soulsa. 5) Barry's Songs I. 6) Theme Player.

http://givnology.ca **for the latest files or to contact us**

Theme Player, Best Loved Classical Themes
ISBN-13: 978-153339672
BISAC: Music / Genres & Styles / Classical

© **Teo (Barry) Vincent IV**

Theme Player
Best Loved Classical Themes

Table of Scores

Some ways to enjoy Theme Player:

Explore melodies that you know and love. Play just the 1st page of Clarinet Concerto. Play Ave Maria's melody and block chords from the guitar chords. In Ave Maria or Laudate Dominum, do the basic version then grab a part from the Trio Score version to embellish it! Explore around and find what's fun!

For the Trio Scores:

The piano part is fully complete in Mozart's 21st Piano Concerto starting at bar 24, just start on page 3! Play the violin melody and piano right hand from Bolero or Winter together. When you have 2 pianos or keyboards, one person can play the bass & violin parts on strings sounds, and the other person, the piano part.

Playing music is the greatest joy, and playing together? Amazing. When we fall in love dancing to "our song" together it is because some musicians put messages in the music that are things we can not even express except in music! Moving to music together makes our bodies and even our world performers in the great sound-movement-visual-feeling experience that can only be music.

Even if it is just memories + a friend playing it + who it is dedicated to + how it is being played or other combinations, it is the most immediate and physically impressive form of collective art experience!

L'Inverno (Winter) from Quattro Stagioni (The 4 Seasons)

Antonio Vivaldi 1678-1741
2016 0901 © Teo (Barry) Vincent IV

L'Inverno (Winter) from Quattro Stagioni (The 4 Seasons) P.2

Baroque trills start on the note above

Chamber Concerto in D major, RV 93

Antonio Vivaldi (1678-1741)

* The Em6 chord is much easier than C#m7b5 and effectively the same

Chamber Concerto in D major, RV 93 (2)

(Follow the bass clef chords)

Baroque trills start on the note above

Baroque trills start on the note above

Gelido in Ogni Vena
from the opera Farnace

Antonio Vivaldi (1678-1741)
(c) 2011 Givnology

Farnace (play by Antonio Maria Lucchini), Music: Antonio Vivaldi 1678-1741

Gelido in ogni vena scorrer mi sento il sangue, l'ombra del figlio enangue m'ingombra di terror.

I feel my blood like ice coursing through every vein. The shade of my lifeless son afflicts me with terror.

Gelido in Ogni Vena (2)

Gelido in Ogni Vena (3)

Che Farò Senza Euridice?

Andante con moto

Christoph Willibald Gluck 1714-1787
Theme Reduction (c) 2014 Teo Vincent IV

Aria del Piacere, Il Trionfo del Tempo e del Disanganno
Pleasure's Aria, The Triumph of Truth and Time

George Frederic Handel
1685-1789 (c) 2011 Givnology

Aria del Piacere, Il Trionfo del Tempo e del Disanganno 2

Aria del Piacere
Lascia la spina, cogli la rosa, tu vai cercando il tuo dolor. Canuta brina, per mano ascosa, guingera quando nol crede il cor.
Pleasure's Aria
Leave the thorn, pluck the rose, you are seeking your own sorrow. An unseen hand will bring you hoary old age ere your heart imagines.

Les Baricades Misterieuses

Francois Couperin 1668-1733

Clarinet Concerto in A Major

Adagio

Wolfgang Amadeus Mozart (1756-179

Piano Reduction (c)2011 05 Teo Vincent IV

Clarinet Concerto in A Major page 2

Laudate Dominum

Andante ma un poco sostenuto

Vesperae Solemnes de Confessore KV 339

Wolfgang Amadeus Mozart (1756-1791)

Re-Adaption (c) 2011 Givnology

The Priest's Aria
Sarasthro's Aria from The Magic Flute

Wolfgang Amadeus Mozart 1856-1891
Freeboards & Vocal arrangement (c) Teo Vincent IV

Ave Maria / Ellens Gesang

Opus 52 #6

Franz Schubert (1797-1828)
Layout (c) 2011 Givnology

Entr'acte de Rosamonde

Franz Schubert 1797-1828
© 2015 Teo Vincent IV

Andantino

Symphony #9 Andante moderato

Andante moderato

Ludwig Van Beethoven
(c) 2013 Teo Vincent IV

Notturno, String Quartet No. 2 in D, 3rd Movement

Andante cantabile ed espressivo

Alexander Borodin 1833-1887
2016 0402 Teo (Barry) Vincent IV

Notturno, String Quartet No. 2 in D, 3rd Movement 2

Bizet Symphony #1 Adagio

Georges Bizet 1838-1875

Adagio ♩=60

This A is optional

Casta Diva

from the opera **Norma**, Opus 61

Vincenzo Bellini (1801-1835)
(c) Givnology 2011

Andante sostenuto assai

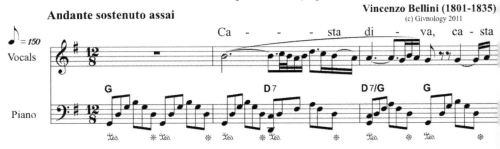

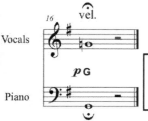

Casta Diva, Norma's aria from the opera Norma

Casta Diva, che inargenti	O pure Goddess, who silver
queste sacre antiche piante,	These sacred ancient plants,
a noi volgi il bel sembiante	Turn thy beautiful semblance on us
senza nube e senza vel...	Unclouded and unveiled...

Translation by Stefano Olcese (solces@tin.it)

Song To The Moon

from the opera Rusalka

Antonin Leopold Dvorak
(1841-1904)

Bars 6 and 14 Cb/Ab can be thought of as Abm7

Romeo And Juliet Overture

Pyotr Ilytch Tchaikovsky (1840-1893)

Andalucia from Suite Española

Ernesto Lecuona 1895-1963
(c) 2011 Givnology

This page is intentionally left blank

Carmen's Habanera
from "Carmen" Op. 21 no. 2

Allegretto quasi andantino

Georges Bizet (1838-1875)

Carmen's Habanera 2

Carmen's Habanera 3

This page is intentionally left blank

Komm Zigany (Come Gypsy)

From the 1924 operetta Princess Maritza

Emmerich Kalman (1882-1953)

2016 0901 © Teo (Barry) Vincent IV

Komm Zigany (Come Gypsy) 4

Komm Zigany (Come Gypsy) 5

Komm Zigany (Come Gypsy) 7

This page is intentionally left blank

Laudate Dominum
Vesperae Solemnes de Confessore K339

Andante ma un poco sostenuto

Wolfgang Amadeus Mozart (1756-1791)

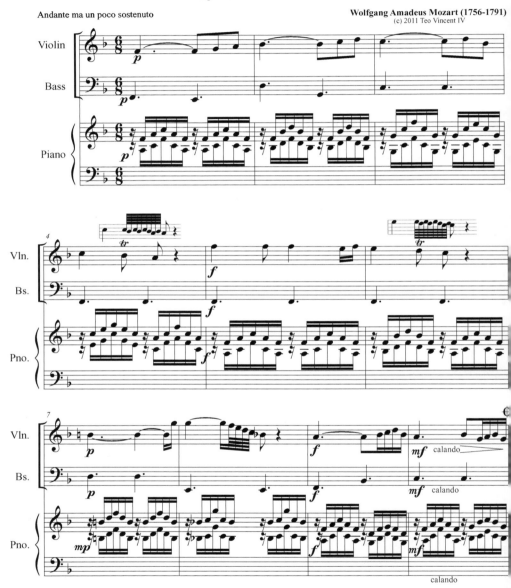

Laudate Dominum 2

Laudate Dominum 3

Laudate Dominum 4

Mozart's 21st Piano Concerto

Andante

Wolfgang Amadeus Mozart 1756-1791

Mozart's 21st Piano Concerto(p2)

Mozart's 21st Piano Concerto(p3)

Mozart's 21st Piano Concerto(p4)

Mozart's 21st Piano Concerto(p5)

Mozart's 21st Piano Concerto(p6)

Mozart's 21st Piano Concerto(p7)

Mozart's 21st Piano Concerto(p8)

Mozart's 21st Piano Concerto(p9)

Sergei Rachmaninoff PC2 Adagio Opus 18

Sergei Rachmaninoff
Trio Score @ Teo Vincent IV 2013

Sergei Rachmaninoff PC2 Adagio page 2

Sergei Rachmaninoff PC2 Adagio page 4

Sergei Rachmaninoff PC2 Adagio page 6

Sergei Rachmaninoff PC2 Adagio page 8

Sergei Rachmaninoff PC2 Adagio page 9

Sergei Rachmaninoff PC2 Adagio page 10

Sergei Rachmaninoff PC2 Adagio page 11

This page is intentionally left blank

Bolero, from the ballet Fandango
Opus M. 81

Tempo di Bolero, moderato assai

Maurice Ravel (1875-1937)
(c) 2011 Teo Vincent IV

Bolero, from the ballet Fandango 2

Bolero, from the ballet Fandango 3

Bolero, from the ballet Fandango 4

Bolero, from the ballet Fandango 5

This page is intentionally left blank

Ave Maria (Ellens Gesang) for Trio

Franz Schubert & Franz Liszt

Trio arrangement (c) 2011 Teo Vincent IV

Lento assai - very slowly

Ave Maria (Ellens Gesang) for Trio 3

Ave Maria (Ellens Gesang) for Trio 4

Ave Maria (Ellens Gesang) for Trio 5

Ave Maria (Ellens Gesang) for Trio 6

This page is intentionally left blank

Serenade / Standchen

Moderato **Schwanengesang** D057 no. 4 Opus 134/90 no. 11 **Franz Schubert (1797-1828**

Serenade 2

Serenade 3

Serenade 4

Traumerei
(Dreaming) Op15, No. 7

Robert Schumann (1810-1856)

Traumerei 2

Fruhlingsstimmen
(Voices of Spring) Op. 410

Johann Strauss, Jr. (1825-1899)

Fruhlingsstimmen 2

Fruhlingsstimmen 3

Fruhlingsstimmen 4

I Manifest My Destiny

Chopin-Dyer-Vincent

Frédéric Chopin's Mazurka in C, Wayne Dyer's book Manifest Your Destiny, Teo Vincent's sense of humor.

ChopinMadeAWay

Chopin-Vincent

Let It Be's

Liszt-Vincen
2008 1128

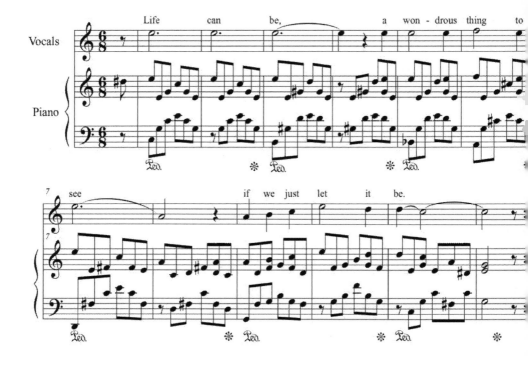

Vocals / Piano

Life can be, a won - drous thing to
see if we just let it be.

Havah Nagilah Chords in Modes:
(this way you can then play it in any key!)

{V V V V i i V-iv V} *fine*
{V V iv iv iv iv V-iv V}
i i i-iv6 i-iv6
{i-i7 VI-i} {iv6-V7 iv6}
Vø V7 i i D.C. al *fine*

Glossary of Italian Music Terms for Virtuoso Performance Ability

a tempo: in time

Adagio brillante: Slowly with brilliance

Allegretto cantabile: cheerfully, in a singing style

Allegro capriccioso: lively & playful

Allegro con brio: with brilliance

Allegro con molto ritmico: with a lot of rhythm

Allegro giusto: steady timing

Allegro vivace: lively

Andante cantibile: in a singing style

Andante, tempo giusto: strict, exact time

Andantino placido: moderate & tranquil

brillante: with brilliance

con spirito: with spirit

delicato e amoroso: delicately & lovingly

dolce con espressivo: sweet & expressive

dolce con grazia: sweet & gracefully

dolcissimo: very sweet

Furioso: furiously

Giocoso: playful

Grandioso e scherzando: grandly & playfully

legato, ma con brio: sustained, but with brilliance

Marcato e misterioso: emphasized & spooky

Moderato con affetto: affectionately

Moderato tranquillo

molto ritmico: with much rhythm

piu serioso: more serious

Presto giocoso: quick & playful

ritardando e ritardando: slower & slower

sempre mp: same volume

smorzando: softer and softer

tempo giusto: exact timing

tranquillo: peaceful

Vivace a capriccio: lively and funny

Manufactured by Amazon.ca
Bolton, ON

33439751R00059